Shadowprints

poems

Kim Zabel

Plain View Press, LLC  1101 W. 34th Street, STE 404
www.plainviewpress.net   Austin, TX 78705

Copyright © 2016 Kim Zabel. All rights reserved under International and Pan-American Copyright Conventions. No part of this book may be reproduced or distributed in any form or by any means, or stored in a database or retrieval system, without written permission from the author. All rights, including electronic, are reserved by the author and publisher.

ISBN: 978-1-63210-030-6
Library of Congress Control Number: 2016946848

Cover photo by Gary Alan Nelson
Cover design by Pam Knight

Special recognition to Gary Alan Nelson, whose nature photography in his book, *Wild Minnesota*, inspired 23 poems in this collection. Those poems are matched with the page of the photo in a list at the back of this book. The cover photograph inspired the poem, "Encroachment at Sea Level, Higher Ground is No Safer" on page 14.

We Find Healing In Existing Reality

Plain View Press is a 36-year-old issue-based literary publishing house. Our books result from artistic collaboration between writers, artists, and editors. Over the years we have become a far-flung community of activists whose energies bring humanitarian enlightenment and hope to individuals and communities grappling with the major issues of our time—peace, justice, the environment, education and gender. This is a humane and highly creative group of people committed to art and social change. The poems, stories, essays, non-fiction explorations of major issues are significant evidence that despite the relentless violence of our time, there is hope and there is art to show the human face of it.

To Dad

Donald C. Hicks
1949-2016

*May these poems find you
at peace in eternity*

Acknowledgements

Gratitude to the publications where these poems have previously appeared:

"Desertion," *Poetography*, The Seventh Collaboration of Photography and Poetry, Crossings at Carnegie, 2012.

"Encroachment at Sea Level, Higher Ground is No Safer," *The Green Blade*, Rural America Writers' Center, Winter 2007.

"Forest Greetings," *The Green Blade*, Rural America Writers' Center, Summer 2006.

"Forming a Triangle, Unconnected," *EDGZ*, No. 12, 2006.

"Homeland," *Albatross*, No. 18, 2007.

"Judas Iscariot," *Four Rivers Review*, 2007.

"Obscured by What Could Be," *Poetography*, The Fifth Collaboration of Photography and Poetry, Crossings at Carnegie, 2010.

"Pharisee," *Four Rivers Review*, 2007.

"Rapture," *Avocet: A Journal of Nature Poems*, Fall 2006.

"Shadowprints," *EDGZ*, No. 12, 2006.

"To Decide What Stays, What Goes," *Four Rivers Review*, 2007.

CONTENTS

Acknowledgements — 4

WATERSONG — 7

Forming a Triangle, Unconnected — 9
Obscured by What Could Be — 11
First Person Plural Forms — 12
Once Water, Trees Reflect in Ice — 13
Encroachment at Sea Level, Higher Ground Is No Safer — 14
One Chance: Immutable, Unforgiving, Without — 15
Both Contain Large Amounts of Precipitation — 16
Watersong — 18

SHADOWPRINTS — 21

Subterrain — 23
To Decide What Stays, What Goes — 24
Beloved Obstacle — 28
Desertion — 29
Wild Genesis and Subtle Trickery — 31
Running Down — 32
Underneath What Appears To Be Land — 33
Shadowprints — 34

WHOLELIGHT — 35

Prodigal — 37
Prodigal Conversation, Years Later — 40
Judas Iscariot — 42
Pharisee — 45
Garden of Gethsemane — 48
The Angel, Gabriel, From Heaven Came — 54
Loose-Bound Notebook, Title Page Forgiveness — 57
Wholelight — 64

HOMELAND   67

    Invitation   69
    Forest Greetings   70
    Rapture   71
    Ground Level   72
    Light Travel   73
    Sanctuary   74
    Birthright   75
    Homeland   76

Special Recognition   77
About the Author   79

WATERSONG

Forming a Triangle, Unconnected

I.

I have been waiting for direction and decision,
wondering if we share a common goal, a common destination.
It has become the fork between us,
yet we are not sharing food from the same plate,
not looking at the landscape from distinguishable viewpoints.
Your glance is clear yet tunneled; mine wide open but underwater,
waving between glints of sunlight and droplets of dew.
You tell me perspective will wipe the fog from the glass,
yet I am the only one drinking from a clear cup,
you, mouth open, gulp water in pure bursts.
You tell me that water should not be contained,
water should not be viewed from behind a window.

II.

Clouds form an arrow, pointing to your side of the stream,
obviously your way is approved by forces beyond us both.
Even the pines, triangle upon triangle, are hedging bets,
leaning up and over to what has now been designated yours.
My smaller sidestream is smoother, quieter, but you tell me
no one values such things anymore. We all want
the furious ride home, the vocal extroverted rage,
who has time for trickle, trickle, soft spot on the rock?
You say this takes millions of years,
a steady evolution far inferior to fast progress.
You tell me to go now,
for quick decisions lead to fast outcomes,
why worry about the ominous colors forming in twilight,
why worry about the lack of rain, the brown spots on evergreens,
you say we all end up in the same patch of water in the end.

Obscured by What Could Be

I ask why you hate this weather,
with its gray horizon hues from water to cloud line,
yet more dust blue and silver than dreary,
yet more thick with living than depressed,
so awake with atmosphere and ozone.
I ask you to take an easy breath; you sigh instead.
These colors do not fit your bright and stiffened palette,
these patterns of light fall beneath your usual spectrum,
you neglect so much in the downcast. Look around.
You miss the perfect constellations within
the complementary and the tertiary,
even the moss grows in unpronounceable shades.
You step atop a perfect paintbrush, a delicate drip of red,
raisin drops of mist pearl and sand,
a thousand new vibrancies of orange,
covered up with a new print: yours, a shoe named missing.
You claim it is humid, a sticky-heavy air,
you claim it is oppressive, a lid clamped clean of fresh,
oblivious to the simple auburn leaf clinging to your boot,
the stem and spine speaking from underneath,
a particle, a piece of precipitation on a drying glove,
a perfectly placed witness wrapped in awe,
a simple pleading to see without despair.

First Person Plural Forms

We are all these fragments of ice,
gripping the rock edge, the glue of each other,
so afraid of falling, melting into a vapor of thin air.
We are all these fragments,
muttering proverbs, noting the best way down,
has anyone returned from the lake, one asks,
what is it like to be blended together,
what is it like to be so vast? Someone must know.
We are all these answers from the rock edge,
forming larger groupings,
devising strategies to eradicate direct sunlight.
We are all in agreement:
winter is too short a season,
who needs this warm body of fusion,
who cares that it keeps a steady current flow,
who really wants an individual snowflake
changed into a simple spell of precipitation?
We are so astutely aware that we unify, later,
when we are not terrified of becoming an other.

Once Water, Trees Reflect in Ice

We know the ache of the frost-covered trees,
know why they lean toward frozen water,
drawing in hope for thaw. This is a simple quenching,
an ice-laden road with a furious beat of prayer,
relief from a dim-lighted hibernation.
We know without it, we all freeze.
But even water must change,
in depth, in temperature, in consistency,
each passing leaves a trail,
each touch, a finger, a brush of the arm,
marking where we have been.
Such similar energies also erode as skin forms new layers,
removes itself from its moist and temporary nest,
and, at that same interval, snow drifts onto ice,
never departing from itself, yet forming its own;
a marriage, a friendship with intertwining boundaries.
We are that water, that ice.

Encroachment at Sea Level, Higher Ground Is No Safer

I am not overtaken by this anomaly, not yet by this iceberg covering.
Where it touches becomes brittle, shrouded and ungreen;
this is a no-fault conversion.
I am waiting for the warming trend, the receding transition
back to its murky flowing; then it will whittle away at rocks,
at seastems, at patches of moss, calling itself sand.
For now, I bask in the oddity of it, the aesthetic.
It is pretty to some, but pain usually is.
Oppression has its own earmark,
the sky bends down to right the fallen
and eventually ice will crack at my feet,
slink away, becoming unlike the mountain, yet similar to,
because even mountains lie down in slow spells.
Be forewarned: this ice is not a blanket, a shroud, a protection;
this is more of an intrusion into an already bitter moment,
an attempt to clamor together when solitude is best.
There is love to be had for the frozen,
just not so close to the sustaining bonebranch.
Keep your distance, keep your blankets to yourself.
Fuel the tundra world and call it beautiful.
Let us see who walks on your earth,
let us see who survives without the blessing and bend of sky.

One Chance: Immutable, Unforgiving, Without

Serenity is hard work.
You are unaware erosion is involved,
no forethought given to current, droplets, particles of air.
Happenings occur in blinks and seconds,
rushing marks of every day into Neptune years.
You revere the solitude, the quiet, the tranquility
provided by constant undermovements.
You say it is nice to have that pause,
even though nothing has really stopped
burgeoning and more is being made.
You observe the contrast of silver on gray,
while ignoring the true rules.
It's a simple magic trick,
that hum of the water, that illusion in sound,
all of it a mask of unrelenting, unceasing,
unpredictable patterns defined.
You want to carve your name in this peace of mind,
stamp your symbol into something hard and permanent,
create a new form, a new you.
You better get busy:
to do this requires the very second
sacrificed to think it;
that idea has now washed downstream
into a bigger tributary.
There is no next time here.

Both Contain Large Amounts of Precipitation

I.

The water is a hue of purple darker, all else is identical.
So much the opposite from real life where similarities
hide beneath bared teeth and clenched eyes shut.
Here, questions emerge, if you turn upside down,
could you tell the difference? Would you know water from sky?
Maybe from this perspective the water simply carries fog
in its arms, maybe the storm is coming from elsewhere.
It can happen, these reversals. But nobody mentions these shifts.

II.

Waking takes place at the usual too-early time,
coffee is poured, papers are read, shoes are tied.
The acknowledgement that the reverse is true never transpires.
Assumptions are our gravity here; bodies of water
don't just turn around overnight. But sometimes
what you thought was upright and proper was merely a negative,
a reverse image, a wrong direction.
How things can change once the pages turn. Look,
how similar we are; the only difference is the reflection,
a distortion of what makes our composition distinct.

Watersong

I.

You say yes.
An optimistic, headlong strut,
determined to change the parameters.
You seem an undefeatable cycle;
proof becomes your mantra and provision.
You do not conquer by ambush,
instead you prefer a methodical rhythm,
a street dance of false hope.
You never offer a choice to decline.
Those heralding the inevitable,
implore you to relinquish your efforts,
save your energy, they say, accept this as is,
draw peace from what will be.

II.

You say no.
Acquiescence is for the weak,
acceptance is the white flag of defeat,
your energy is drawn from this struggle,
and you will rethink those very words.
But look around, they say,
you are surrounded by your own future,
others have gone the solid path.

III.

You say not yet.
This moment will not be vanquished
for something as meager as doubt.
Some laws cannot be defied, they say, and you agree.
Yet you are governed by persistent force,
your nature is to move uphill, break solid ground,
killing and curing within the same movement.
No one should underestimate you:
you turn mountains into sand.

SHADOWPRINTS

Subterrain

Tell me where you live when you are not here
among the clattering of spoons and ideas,
among the busy day-in, night-out of lusts and reprimands,
tell me about the place that is so much better than this,
the place where three moons rise at night,
grass stretches to touch the soft side of your ankle,
even a local planet is known to nod at your brilliance,
even the velvet prince makes a fresh path in the woods.
Tell where you live when you are not here
when sentinel spirits guard holy rings of age,
where the earth looks glorious in all its hues of lush,
where veins have voice, where rocks found deep
hold the very connections to the creator,
bought only with savage pain and salt apology,
bought only with vicarious sacrifice and bloodletting.
Here, you say, no one dares to bargain with the divine.

To Decide What Stays, What Goes

I.

Plans take shape in the shade of a long sitting oak tree;
sporadic weeds are not necessarily
the vegetation that should be plucked.
To remove what appears to be mold-slimed
and sullied can also take away
benign and prosperous growth.
Leave it for later pruning,
leave it for the mindful plantings.

II.

Find small respite in dandelions;
take refuge underneath stem,
underneath the soft floppy bend of breeze.
To peel a scab in the earth of old wounds
opens the center,
the blood of your actions
moves to the corners,
taking the skin of the very ground.
Rehealing begins,
knowing the sad benefit of a fading scar.

III.

Do not suggest the trajectory here;
untying an old laced shoe
proves an all-morning task.
This is lopsided,
to wear peace like a mask,
while sliding the sickle into sifted
wheat behind the backs of neighbors.
All that is cut down
simply reflects an emptiness,
that egoism of personal fear.

IV.

Some openings should be left untouched;
their hinges firmly shut.
No law claims every piece of soil
should be uncovered and exposed,
even if it is easy to dispel,
even if the light from underneath
shines with brilliance and opportunity.
That very light deconstructs,
scours the surface of a much-needed rain.

Beloved Obstacle

Your cleverings have failed,
as have your scrapings,
your clawings,
your throwing devices,
all those clefts and crevices
carved through persistence.
You only beautify through battery,
add, not subtract,
only reveal the tender,
medium-rare middle,
so gorgeous at sunset.
I admire your tenacity,
your maneuverings to and fro,
it is too bad we do not have
a common foe.
But for now, I am that fixture forcing
expansion, that bullheaded boulder
I demand that you brush against,
circle, entwine. For now,
I am that stubborn structure,
that constant impervious nerve,
that power that makes you want
to move me.

Desertion

I.

You have left us here yet call us beautiful.
You believe that abandonment is attractive
to those who enjoy repair, reconciliation of the lost.
You think it is easy to cross the thickness of water,
believing what lies beneath is shallow land.
Your goal is to climb upon the boulder and stand,
admire how lovely it is above,
making sure this is only a visitation,
a vacation from the common ground.
You believe abandonment is a sanctuary
to those who make sport of finding,
righting apparent wrongs in full sweeps,
you ask if we are glad to be comforted.
What you cannot do is make clamor a gift it is not.
You are better off not breaching the divide between us.
We are fine here without divine intervention,
without field reports and analysis, without you,
paving the way to ethereal regions,
plunking your heavy tools into us,
motorizing your way to heaven.

II.

You have found us hidden and claim ownership,
yet we are not yours.
Just because you have ripped away the gentle covering,
scoured the path with righteous cleansing,
does not allow you to borrow.
Any removal is pure theft, a mishandling
of a place you left for better. Leave the abandoned
to those who would prefer to stumble upon brilliance,
to those who are not gutting open the land
and leaving it without assistance.
So beautiful, you say, the dark blood clumping,
coagulating, so unfamiliar with hungry oxygen,
so beautiful, you say, as its organs twitch,
thrash in each last movement.
You are in awe, a witness to this,
you, with eyes open, noting with hands
in your pockets, with knife ready for more.

Wild Genesis and Subtle Trickery

This is the precipice of majesty,
eliciting so many colors, all distinct.
This is an ongoing present tense,
an act of creation,
each movement drawing itself,
reaching to another beside itself.
The water knows this purposeful overture,
this together chord,
a curious dimension stops to listen,
yet no trace of its presence is found.
Its nature is to transfer blame to those
convinced they simply lost track of it,
yet wasn't it the warning of the wolf prints
and not the owl in the distance
that sent clues of these patterned moments?
Stand still, something is emerging here,
muted by the awe of landscape.
Be clever like the wolf,
like mystery and water,
like all who can make new.

Running Down

Soft high grass grasps at memory, at bare legs,
at the promise never to forget the sensation.

Arms outstretched like hawk wings, like flight,
yet loving the very ground too much to leave.

Greeting the markings of a distant tree, of childish
correspondences, pretending to know the language.

Using the wind as breath, as a calling voice,
listening to the soft open words planted into the land.

Each step a small destruction, an intrusion,
yet each step closer to a river only requesting repentance.

Trying to form vowels, to translate an ancient dialect,
aware that communion always becomes a silent exchange.

Knowing that when destination meets the walking current,
all previous inhabited space will have already changed.

Peering backwards at once-was, at the distance disguised,
into the unfamiliar winged journey downstream.

Underneath What Appears To Be Land

Patterns of particles form snow shadows
just below eye level,
and no footstep dares to cross
such an unriddled, unmired path,
even the birds have yet to touch down here.
Sometimes the snow forbids it,
signals its warnings through the tapestry of light,
striping the earth in gray and purple,
each line spelling the silence of morning.
This way, the day begins pure.
It is best not to trample this supple space,
it is best not to invade the trespass
between open and dense,
between leap and air.
Never assume the absence of the watchful,
shackled and sparse in this vacuum of pure dawn.
The lack of movement is no guarantee,
even stifled breath makes a noise,
changes the amplitude of temperature,
of vapor traveling unseen from one space to the next.
Tread carefully, listen to the mutable crunch of snow
just beneath. It is the loudest echo,
no matter how transparent the step.

Shadowprints

Your shadow is a footprint on the forest floor,
and some of your handprints
still remain on the thick trunks.
Shadows usually do not linger alone in space,
and when they do, you say it is a worrisome event.
It is then they are no longer shadows,
it is then they become the once-known.
Heavy, tricky trees line up in neat rows,
sway in an unified direction, pretending to mark a path outward.
There is no real path, just a road to lostness,
there are no real shadows, just the searching
for the once-resembled, looking for someone to silhouette.
You combat these fears with superstitions,
never stepping on the sun and only touching
the top of every third rock.
You say it's tedious, being chased by footprints
not made by the known.
You say some superstitions still hide in the woods,
clashing with your new fears as you walk past.
One false belief meets another and both dislike each other,
a brewing ensues; this is how shadowprints are made,
this is why the markings in the clay
are pointing in multiple directions,
each step a frantic heel-toe pulse saying,
which way, which way, which way.

WHOLELIGHT

Prodigal

I.

Why reach for me,
I am nothing more than a despised crust;
there is nothing to be gained.
So many boundless gifts presented,
a continual conversation,
a desire that we correspond,
yet my words are of such little importance,
a simple speckle of water in an evaporating pool.
I clamor to the front porch and knock softly,
an unspoken request from a simple second-chancer,
a lukewarm variety. When you answer,
the door opens wide, celebratory-style. Come, you say,
while lighting candles and bringing the best wine.
My shaky and parched fingers circle this new glass;
hold and behold,
you are in perfect company,
sit and be safe.

II.

My past place consumes so much tugging and pulling.
I have wallowed too long at the foot of the root tree,
hoping to be sustained. Its sap provided initial nourishment,
yet I remained in stubborn allegiance to dead undergrowth.
Simple enchantment by wolves and elves convinced me
they would make better friends.
The magic and the hunt, so appealing on first journey step,
so wearying when it wears threadbare.
The dance with fire is slow, monotonous, and horrifying.
Sometimes hungry wolves eat their own.
Sometimes the elves paint quicksand in the forest floor.
Sometimes once the bait is caught,
sinking wide-eyed and wailing,
the arms still able to flail at the once-never friends,
the wolves lick their lips.
This, think no more of it;
this, you would never do.

III.

You knew about the quicksand and the quick tongues
and sent sentinels to protect me from the arms of windfall.
You knew about the lure of the low-notes,
the danger of squander;
the large wildebeests in the open field were the least of my concerns.
It is always the irresistible,
the attractive, those are the true devils.
Evil never comes as itself,
who would follow such a snarly, gaping desperation?
It comes without a knock, unannounced, smiling.
You, between the knockless point,
between the sentinels and prayer,
awaited my arrival, prodigal style,
outstretched, with voice calling above the competitive wind,
a breeze of nuanced you:
please, join me, I have been waiting.

I am so happy, at last, with you home.

Prodigal Conversation, Years Later

I.

She says:

After returning home from a journey into feedlots and harlots,
into pig manure and feverish desert,
the black velvet pouch was gambled away at temples of nonrefusal.
Understanding of these simple concepts:
bereft and broke;
this is what led to the sanctity of here.
Still, a meal is prepared; the wine-dance is poured.
This celebration speaks of new health,
like the creeping away of a cough.
Yet praising the cure diminishes the celebration of already well-being,
the current good.
Always overlooked and expected,
these cheers strike the present hardest in the face.

II.

He says:

Lump your clay into mine,
make a bowl in which our soup and wine are always replenished,
always plentiful, always bound by mercy.
Your pace, in rhythm with my trodden step,
never strays from my presence:
this is cause for the highest generosity.
Boundaries between our beings do not curve us apart.
They hold in a holy union, undefiled by the stretch of otherness,
by the stretch of singularity.
My offerings are humble,
unworthy of your lack of wanderlust.
Truly, this is what we celebrate tonight:
the lack of departure,
the absence of squander;
this delight is more than any return could purchase.

Judas Iscariot

I.

Impaled on betrayal, that rugged wilderness,
that particular landscape holds such initial charm.
Yet, not even a day later,
each step becomes a lost and painful hollow,
movement hurts the very ground.
Those wild walls are lined with blunt branches;
it is not the sharp clean pierce that injures
but the dull heavy punch that never numbs.
This is why some hang from self-made yokes,
this is why some walk straight into the water,
singing a pale lullaby mixed with subtle laughter
and twig-in-the-lung gasps against such stale air.

II.

No one anticipates this route.
No map outlines the trajectory here;
even the ripped-in-spots parchment put together
with strong and meaningful tape
does not include this unbidden subtext.
Imagine land intruding and demanding payment,
knowing betrayal is the worst remorse.
So much is lost in the itching and cutting;
who can shed enough skin to pay what is owed?
Rawness is not enough compensation.
Hence the lullaby, later, after miles of what if,
after years of almost.

III.

Such obvious markings this place leaves on its visitors:
the treading and pacing,
the damp aura,
the scaly mutterings,
the try-too-hard hug:
all is spoken with that glance-look-away.
Then, that very silence, it circles around forgetfulness,
lusting for it like the content of an adolescent lovesong.
This is the bargain made with betrayal:
there is no forgetting,
only a deeper remembrance,
a picking apart of events like a scab,
an unhealed wound with nothing to show
but a few coins and some dried pus.

Pharisee

I.

How great thou art: this is your selfsong,
repeated as a mantra;
exalted before the most high,
placed above the divine.
Your absence against this pure sacristy deceives:
the holiest shrine is without uncertainty.
You cannot live among omniscience
so ragged and defiled,
so covered in snot.
Even the best attempts at beauty never lift above ground.
Yet you refuse to acknowledge your presence
in the ocean of dead skin,
refuse to admit that your answers
are superimposed and fault-filled,
refuse to wipe your mouth on a clean-covered cloth.
All of this becomes unshackled condemnation,
your fiercest ally.

II.

Contriteness is upheld for all to see;
look at my humility,
repeat it to those who appear to be unworthy of banquet halls.
Stay in the soup kitchen.
Look at how benevolent, how generous.
You fill the coffers with your blood-stained coins,
waiting for people to ask about the pain of giving,
the sacrifice of your own self-worth.
White-washed and foolhardy,
gifts are wrapped in the finest silk paper;
inside a swarm of dust and beetles
feast on your delusions that good works will achieve paradise.

III.

Speak the asking price, you say,
demand it from an omnipotent force,
any one of them will do your bidding.
Think and it will become.
Think highly of yourself for being able to think
so highly of yourself.
Such power, you claim, while showering the altar
with incense and waving those pawny arms mid-air.
Cats disappear, as do rabbits from hats,
put-together women are then split in half,
the trap door is sleek and prepared,
such smoke and mirrors here, that fantastic show.
You say you can clear the scabs from the leper's hand,
yet your indulgence in self-adulation has excluded two basic laws:
never forget to honor the maker of ringed planets and prisms,
of quark-fusion, of morning halo.
And never.
Never claim divinity unless fish and loaves multiply in your hand,
unless demons flee from your presence,
unless water becomes wine by word alone.

Garden of Gethsemane

I.

You rub undernourished sticks against a hope
this whittling will produce an other-than cold;
a below zero dusk knocks on your snowfloor:
hurry before it arrives.
Adrenaline will not scour this plague of ice,
neither will the sticks,
now dampened with your own furies;
lost now, precious heat emitted by particles of dew.
Gloves could be removed to garner a quicker fire:
a counterintuitive gesture,
the dogs pace and whine,
yet sit upright at the coming of the nightnoon.
It is almost here.

II.

Numb gloves and sweat mixed with sour snow sticks:
such a lack of provisions.
Your grayblue lips could once belly-up
conversations of heartiness and infallibility,
yet so quiet now,
moving only to taste the chapped blood,
the loose skin,
those inborn moments of willpower and panic.
A new concern now for the placement of flames.

III.

Step forward a minute and find other wood.
Two sticks alone burn quickly,
the night methodically moves towards.
The dogs do not worry you will use them as kindling;
yet thoughts rise from your numbing, stark-weary synapses.
Maybe the sled, a thought slows and stops there,
worth one night of warmth and a footwalk to safety.
The night shadows up to the door,
yet you are not ready.

IV.

The head of one dog lowers to the ground.
Heavy weather and coat, fingers and sticks:
the difference between the two and the four.
Small tokens of warmth,
those wood charmers chided and cavorted,
you, now shrouded in the unsealable night.
Transparent travelers taunt with ghost hands,
foreshadowing your own ground.
Mired here in the wood,
only visible when light decides night wins.

V.

Wool, flannel, a water-resistant top coat,
a leather watch strapped to your wrist:
all talismans now.
Time announces
your presence in the snowdark.
Yet is a looming word,
one that carries many threads,
an extra blanket of despair.
And, then, the wait.

VI.

Then, the prayer.
An odd request of one compelled:
not for warmth, for fire, for a snowless ground,
not for provisions of material.
Not for survival,
for safety of fingers and toes,
for oxygen and a steady step.
Not for protection from that opaque hunger;
your own dogs may turn on you for meat.
Instead, your prayer reflects the snow
in the drops of blood on your brow;
instead, your prayer smooths over
the icy stones in your heels;
instead, your prayer:
a bony-humble please be near.

The Angel, Gabriel, From Heaven Came

I.

A mere three hours,
a mere handsbreath before giving birth,
a recollection of events from that place
with the pointed stone to the watershore.
Uncommon is unfitting vocabulary,
yet not impossible considering your constitution.
You have always known that exaltation
should never originate from its owner;
the fall from grace is a long one,
a pit of stomach-in-throat experience,
a flat landing onto soiled ground.
To lift, to levitate, others need to blow smooth air
underneath your very soles;
only then and with a nod from grandness.
True humility is the divine
walking among you in the temple courts.

II.

You have always known
that the convergence of intervention and refusal
often results in whaleblood and plankton,
in roaming five desert floors
with parched throat and ripped-at-the-arch feet,
causing each hamstring to yawn.
Sorrow lodges in the sternum,
a devotion unwilling.
No provisions exist:
a simple absence of an entrance point.
You only need to ask.
Do not fashion an answer.
Paste the asking on rock walls for others:
an arrow marking.

III.

Yet you did not refuse:
chosen just as humility argues against logic.
Your prayers are remembered and kept sacred,
the handstitched book with the gilded ledgings,
the coarse drawstring, the heavy binding.
Written there are simple solaces from sharp rocks aimed
at the gentle underpart of arm and requests for more words.
You remembered an angel,
so deeply bathed in golden light
that you could see wingless air afoot.
Most highly favored, most highly favored:
your step in place beat of heart.
It is both memory and prayer.

Loose-Bound Notebook, Title Page Forgiveness

I.

Seventy times seven:
we have been redeemed for those failings.
Those outstanding griefs pounded into wood and flesh,
exposed the sinewy lacings of vein and bone.
Here, the ultimate gift, with no requirements to respond.
What has been so freely wrapped and sealed,
discarded by the tenant of anger and fear.
Those are fighting words now.

II.

For those who lash with cat-o-nine tails,
for those unwilling to lift the heaviness
of what has been carried so long,
for those whose spit is dried to legs and fingers,
receive this gift.
Indeed, there are other options,
opportunities to handpick a wide-marbled road,
so smooth and cool to the heels,
such an easier resort.
Look closely, though, at this other way,
this little dirt spell in the grove,
this one will not abruptly end at your death.

III.

A few things are known:
multiplication of kindness, an example set,
a close walk down a now-lighted path.
Such a long and heavy mile for the already shackled,
for those unwilling to sacrifice even the smallest portion
of bread and water to the beaten man hunched over:
that man is vomiting from dehydration next to the tree.
Such a big request for those of us planted in the earth,
fighting for root space.

IV.

The forces that buckle most knees use simple division.
That particular brand of math costs plenty,
yet what is deserved and the price that is paid
are not truly acquainted.
That sign, above the heads of those who know the difference
between gift and advantage,
pronounces a verdict both shallow and loathsome.
This idea, this taking without return,
without acknowledging the source,
causes such a multiplication of darkness.

V.

Drawn with charcoal and pastel,
with broad strokes and blood,
is a place without salvation.
A standing and open reservation exists there.
Yet you offer a gift so large that most walk right past it,
wondering about that cloudy space in the center of the room.
Those numbers refuse to add up.
Long division appears to rule supreme on this plane.

VI.

You could have called it a day,
a very long hour of trial;
you could have cut your losses early on.
But you didn't.
You decided that seventy times seven
is the least of what should be done.
Without this, you could not multiply what doesn't exist.
Benevolence takes place underneath the division bell
with the deafening sounds of crows echoing the morning.
No one ever expects to find it there.

VII.

That journey to save just one,
the belief that it would be worth it,
that utter contentment with expansion,
with the very miracle you brought,
should be an example to repeat those steps again and again.
Learn how to carry, to borrow,
to cross over when multiplying such long numbers,
such waves of contentment.
Add those many lines together;
check your answers with the provided concordance.
It has already been written.

Wholelight

I.

You are moving the electromagnetic field with each utterance,
with each silence still spoken.
Slowly that field is reversing, or forwarding,
depending on position,
towards ripple and wave,
a piecemeal tsunami.
Your punctuation touches particle upon particle,
what have you done?

II.

In high gravity, no true down exists.
Find yourself in sphere time,
moving ahead of voice,
facing only forward while expectations
freefall ahead without hurrying.
All you believe unties,
scatters into fragments,
like nothing you have ever known.

III.

To make things perfectly clear:
you, matter.
That smirk-low remark, the coarse conscience,
that intent to inactivate,
all reties into wholelight, a canvas complete.
Matter is busy adding these volumes to possibility.
You found forever disarranged
because of a simple shrug,
a nervous two-beat step away, away, away.
Each movement in the wholelight,
without divine intervention,
is linked by small dustings of your own venom.
Self-propulsion still leads towards that singularity.
Your own refusal punches dents into the space fabric,
yet you blame others for these depressions.
Straighten the shallows;
deeper matter will begin to recognize your voice.

HOMELAND

Invitation

Step carefully, watch the overgrowth;
come here, give considerable care to this ledge of rock.
See the falling hum of water, flimsy moss beneath hands,
notice how currents do not crash here, waves bloom instead,
notice the level of green, each portion of pigment,
gratitude always ends a long day of work.
It is a busy-still. Not the ominous forest-found quiet,
but a song in skipping step, a beat of plenty to do,
grass blades swing, arms of the hectic-happy,
every purposeful leaning contains an element of play,
yet everything continues as one same motion,
a pleasant monotony with a northern rhythm.
Sleep is earned and well-deserved when it comes.

Forest Greetings

This is the height of youth,
eight or nine, four feet, and you
nearby circling a wide trunk,
one arm caressing the bark,
the other gathering breeze sing-song style.
I am standing next to a tall puzzle,
each piece looks like a scab to pick,
but I outline it instead, the pattern, the shapes,
I find a face like my own among the intricate design,
this part looks like me, I call out,
if I were wearing a hat. I touch the unevenness,
notice how rubbing it numbs the palm of my hand,
how my skin pales under the exercise.
I begin to circle the trunk, slowly,
feeling each shape like continents,
Africa and Greenland, my favorite look-alikes.
I extend my other hand, my arm to the wind,
hello, I say aloud, as I rotate around faster,
hello, hello, hello,
like a small satellite with a temporary orbit.
I notice that you have not stopped your spinning,
and our trees are close enough that when our orbits coincide,
we come together, open-handed, facing one another.
I gently touch my fingertips to your outstretched palm,
sparking a continuance of tree, you, me, tree,
hello, hello, hello

Rapture

In this quiet country, voice is a gift of the wild,
nothing is deeper than sound.
Here, existence is brutal without wings,
without roots or an additional set of feet.
Notice the ample oxygen on the inhale,
the overwhelming sensation of migration,
notice the only vehicle is a careful canoe.
See how the skin of the land is deep,
see how the beauty travels far beneath it.
This place provides a temporary shelter
from the safety of cities, tight enclosures, hospitals.
Here, if you become prey, if you misstep into ego,
no one will protest the injustice of your death.
This is because you navigated beyond boundaries,
you chose to experience the face of God first hand.
Record your observations in a hard-bound journal
soaked with rainwater and impromptu splashes,
record soon and often, before angels notice
your passageway is not protected by blood.
This is no place for wandering, for getting lost,
there is no challenge in taking the obvious route.
Create a map from your notes, from your daily writings,
trace it twice with your fingertips, commit it to memory.
Hope lies between these lines.

Ground Level

Finally, arrival. A welcomed drenching,
a solstice series tumbling through the clouds
until saturation becomes the ultimate nemesis.
The philandering sun, always visiting, leaving,
loving other places, is replaced by an inferior rock;
the moon is always a bridesmaid.
We toss on a bed of fitful sleep,
sometimes we bend so far north we ache
for balance, sometimes we hide underneath
one another, sometimes we only rest upright.
Tonight, the sun sheds a final glow,
we await the parade of arrows, so showy and striking.
We are lucky not to be immovable stones,
which can never dodge or risk breaking.
We are grateful for flexible spirits, for prairie dances,
for rotations and orbits. Watch carefully:
our sleight of hand manipulates torrents,
impending gusts bow to free-flowing pirouettes,
a smooth grand jeté lands in the middle of winter.
Our grace creates such good here.

Light Travel

I saw your footprints on the water,
steady in some places, skirting rocks,
shifting undercurrents elsewhere,
you learned early to walk on the light.
You told me that once a foot sinks
into darker avenues,
those quiet, solemn gateways,
the ankle quickly becomes wet,
then the whole body falls in,
sliding with the current of fear.
It isn't necessary to tiptoe to remain
upright on the surface,
simply find a sunlit patch and stroll.
This can also be done at night, in rushes,
in heavy tides, in waves, in impossible crossings,
you tell me that I just have to know where to look.
This is the true and difficult task:
it isn't the walking but the placement that matters.
You say I walk all day long on less stable ground,
places prone to give way and shift,
yet when the strength of water is beneath me,
you say I hesitate to move from peak to peak,
not placing my footsteps on the smooth brinks of light.
You say others call your gift miraculous, God-like,
water walking is thought of as an ever-plenty basket of fish,
the newly-healed leper, the raising of the dead.
You say it isn't as complicated as that.
Just watch your step.

Sanctuary

Stillness begets stillness, silence is always a leader,
the laws of entropy still apply in the wild.
Without the frenetic go in this calm,
what remains is be, steadfast being,
only participles and principles of still verbs.
You are solid like this, softening the hard edges
of water, the crash-over and drowning,
the unrelenting goes around, becomes,
melds into you, a desire of being so contained,
so still. Soon, what once was a torrent, a circular
estimation gaining speed, a device ready to topple,
becomes quiet, soothed by your refusal to react,
soothed by your assurance that standing still
is a fortress, an unmitigated strength,
providing the necessary solace
for the wind-strung and weary,
for the hesitant and hunted,
for the roots growing underwater.

Birthright

Let me speak to you about reverence,
my holy ground, my exquisite sense, my visual morning,
an artist would nod eagerly at the spectacle.
Even the rocks, the hardest surfaces,
turned sideways and almost crumpled,
are purposeful and perfect here.
Could you find a better blue? The deep
midnight in broad day meshes with lighter sky,
you are a palette worthy of lingering eyes.
Who is your maker?
Parents who receive high praise for gifted children
are all knowing, reading Milton late into the night,
telling stories of golden goblets and holes in the sky,
listening to the right sequence of rests and whole notes,
creating creatures of genius. You are no different.
Where is your mother? Let me speak to her about managing
the to and fro of you, the waves and distance in thought,
How did she let go enough to let you begin?
Where is your father? Let me speak to him about late nights
in the kitchen, cooking pancake flat rocks in hues of rain,
how does he know which part of him you are?
And where are you? Let me speak to you about majestic order,
your brilliance of textiles layered seven deep,
how do you not realize your own splendor?

Homeland

This is my here, my grounding, my firmament,
where I can feel its presence with each step,
a place revered by ancestors, chosen by family,
a place where the disrespectful are dismissed
with a bootkick elsewhere.
Be intimidated: this is sacred ground.
Yet I am supported here in the unrelenting,
in the changing and unpredictable seasons
because I only borrow the smallest portion
from this place, always grateful for its loan.
I can hear the dialogue of the gravel roads,
the movement underfoot, the stones creating
such careful positions to mark my path home.
These stones know me, know all those before me,
know those who crafted so carefully from its bounty,
gently promising preservation. Any attempt to unhinge
our relationship is carved in these woods
and documented in the silence. This is worth saving,
this is worth loving, this here, this gift of surrounding.

Special Recognition

Special recognition to Gary Alan Nelson, whose nature photography in his book, *Wild Minnesota*, inspired these poems (listed with the page of the photo in *Wild Minnesota*).

"Beloved Obstacle," page 19
"Birthright," page 25
"Both Contain Large Amounts of Precipitation," page 21
"Desertion," page 98
"Encroachment at Sea Level, Higher Ground is No Safer," page 65
"First Person Plural Forms," page 156
"Forest Greetings," page 133
"Forming a Triangle, Unconnected," page 36
"Ground Level," page 155
"Homeland," page 22
"Invitation," page 28
"Light Travel," page 33
"Obscured by What Could Be," page 46
"Once Water, Trees Reflect in Ice," page 38
"One Chance: Immutable, Unforgiving, Without," page 3
"Rapture," page 86
"Running Down," page 6
"Sanctuary," page 107
"Shadowprints," page 20
"Subterrain," page 91
"Underneath What Appears to be Land," page 139
"Watersong," page 100
"Wild Genesis and Subtle Trickery," page 39

About the Author

Kim Zabel was born in Fargo, North Dakota. She moved to Phoenix, Arizona and from there to Albuquerque, New Mexico, where she graduated with a MA from the University of New Mexico. Although she grew up in the Southwest, her extended family resides in Minnesota, and she has always considered it home. She returned to Minnesota in 1996.

This is her first book of poetry, which was made possible by the voters of Minnesota through a grant from the Southeastern Minnesota Arts Council (SEMAC) thanks to a legislative appropriation from the arts and cultural heritage fund.

She writes for two publications: the *Post-Bulletin/507 Magazine* and *Rochester Women*.

www.ingramcontent.com/pod-product-compliance
Lightning Source LLC
Chambersburg PA
CBHW052115070526
44584CB00017B/2492